The Sociology Instructional Design Model

Yolanda El Etan

Published by:
Best Global Publishing Ltd
PO Box 9366
Brentwood
Essex
CM13 1ZT
United Kingdom

www.bestglobalpublishing.com

Table Of Contents

The Birth of the Sociology Instructional Design Model.. 4
Courses...................14
School Description................. 20
Staff....40
Sociology Training Model.... 58

The Sociology Instructional Design Model

Chapter 1

The Birth of The Sociology Instructional Design Model

EQ, IQ, and Social Intelligence

IQ

When I looked up the word IQ, or intelligent quotient, I came across a test that is used to measure a subject's ability to confront situations that they might confront in life. However, Many people think of IQ as a learner's ability to do intellectual or academic tasks. It is the computation of intelligence (Encyclopedia Britannica 2006).

EQ is based on the concept of knowing oneself through emotions before we can learn about others and engage in academic dialog, (Goleman 1985).

The Sociology Instructional Design Model

Goleman tries to connect the emotions to learning, and then allows his discussion to go into social intelligence. For example, you might react to a situation based on your emotions then there is a path to learning. He uses the emotions of fear, happiness and combines these emotions with understanding of ones self and understanding of others as a basis for learning. However it doesn't take one long to realize that this travels into the slope of psychology, sociology that is all social sciences.

Techniques used in teaching EQ are often associated with morals, manners, and etiquette, which are all social. EQ is more appropriate that EQ comes out of the constructivist theories of today. These are similar to Steps 1, 3, 8 of Gagne's Nine Events in the *Principles of Instructional Design* (1979).

The Sociology Instructional Design Model

I just wanted a simple definition of EQ however, upon reading the reviews of Goleman's Emotional Intelligent (1985), the readers picked out what the book was missing. The readers seemed to imply that the concept is too simple. It does travel from EQ into Social Intelligence under the same heading as Emotional Intelligence and they could pick the two concepts apart. This led my research to other instructional technology theories that I have used for a long time. I did not want to get into these theories in this book, however I must mention Gardener as referencing if nothing else. Goleman has written a book on social intelligence, which I have not read.

Gardner in *Frames of Mind: The Theory of Multiple Intelligences* (1983) combined the use of learning centers and hands on learning in his instructional theory. He incorporated the use of fine arts into whole learning. For example, if a child wants to go to music, the child will do to a section of the room that contains only musical resources. All of the theories above lead to the development of *The* Sociology *Instructional Design Model.*

Sociology Instructional Design Model

The social instructional model builds on the creative curriculum and the classical learning models. It incorporates constructivist, behavior, and cognitive learning theories. Learning centers are created using whole rooms instead of spaces. These rooms will be called laboratories. The homeroom is the social awareness room in which children learn character education and emotional intelligence. Children will change classes as early as the age of 5. The social awareness teacher would take the children from laboratory to laboratory. For example, the technology

The Sociology Instructional Design Model laboratory would consist of computers, machines, and could be integrated with mathematics. After school and free time would consist of camps. Children could study what they want to study. This would be referred to as classical training. The main laboratories used would be, math, science, art and physical education.

SQ

Socrates might have been thinking of social intelligence when he said, "I am not Athenian or Greek, but a citizen of the world. Plutarch quotes Socrates in his writings, "On Banishment," from *Plutarch's Morals,* rev. in 1871 by Goodwin, William W. in vol. 3, p. 19. Therefore I have invented the following called the social quotient or SQ: For example, $SQ > IQ$. IQ has no use if it cannot be applied to the world. For example, $IQ < SQ.IQ$ is inside of SQ. For example a child

The Sociology Instructional Design Model cannot become a product of society with a high IQ and no SQ; vice versus if a child can't perform in society it doesn't matter how smart they are. SQ will have an effect or an impact on IQ. For example, $SQ \geq IQ$ and $IQ \leq SQ$. IQ cannot exist without SQ. For example, $SQ=IQ$. Formal education provides one with one or the other. For example, with out the use of social studies we cannot imply the value of IQ. There are instances where the equation doesn't apply, but rarely.

Character education may include the following themes of study. School days, rules, circle time, problem based learning, respect, tolerance, and trustworthiness. This model places emphasis on SQ existing outside of IQ.

Fig 1 SQ formula

The Three R's

Students must take one of READING WRITING and

ARITHMETIC courses every semester.

Reading-World   Literature,   British,   American,

Language, Spanish, French, German, Short Story, and

Novel

The Sociology Instructional Design Model

Writing-Essays, Journals, Book Reports, Grammar, Analysis, Evaluation, and Synthesis.

Critical Writing, Poems, Dictionary, Antonyms, Synonyms, Scripts, Research papers

Arithmetic-Basic Math, Computers, Logic, College Math, Algebra, Geometry, Advanced Math, Business Math, General Math Problems, Trigonometry, Calculus, and Statistics.

IQ *fig 2.Explanation of IQ*

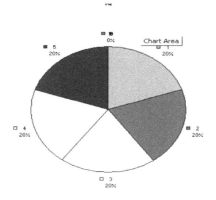

CLASSICAL TRAINING

The following are sample subjects: Art, Vocational Education, Drama, Music, PE, Dance, and Science. Art Subject samples are the following: drawing, design, paint, and sculpture. Physical education subject samples are the following: Soccer, archery, gym, aerobics, T-ball, volleyball, swimming, badminton, tennis, fencing, chess, lacrosse, golf, basketball, football, volleyball, piano, orchestra, and choir. Science subject areas are the following: General science, zoology, earth science, physical science, astronomy, biology, chemistry, geology, physics, botany, meteorology. Sociology is made of EQ and SQ and must exist for the basis of IQ to occur. It surrounds IQ.

The Sociology Instructional Design Model

Chapter 2

Courses

Academic Courses

Reading
World Literature
British Literature
American Literature

Language
Chinese
Arabic
Spanish
French
German
Writing
Short Story Novel
Essays
Journals
Book Reports
Grammar
Analysis
Evaluation
Synthesis
Critical Writing
Poems
Dictionary
Antonyms
Synonyms
Scripts
Research papers

Arithmetic
Basic Math
Computers
Logic
College Math
Algebra
Geometry
Advanced
Math,
Business math
General Math Problems
Trigonometry
Calculus
Statistics

Classical Courses

Classical courses consist of the following; Classical Languages, Art, Vocational Education, Drama, Music, PE, Dance, Science. These courses will be studied as part of before and after school curriculum and during camps. Camps occur in the summer and during school breaks.

Hinrichs, Fritz (2006) in Introduction to classical education states:

Many people refer to classical Education as Christian education, but in this discussion I will only rely on two portions of the discipline, Trivium and the second, the Quadrivium.

The Trivium contained three areas; Grammar, Dialectic, and Rhetoric. Each of these three areas was specifically suited to the stages in a child's mental development. During his early years a child studies the Grammar portion of the Trivium. The Grammar period (ages 9-11) includes a great deal of language, preferably an ancient language, such as Latin or Greek, that will require the child to spend a great deal of time learning and memorizing its' grammatical structure. During their younger years children possess a great natural ability to memorize large amounts of material even though they may not understand its significance. This is the time to fill them full of facts, such as the multiplication table, geography, dates, events, plant and animal classifications; anything that lends itself to easy repetition and assimilation by the mind. During the second period, the Dialectic period (ages 12-14), the child begins to understand that which he has learned and begins to use his reason to ask questions based on the information that he has gathered in the grammar stage. The third period Sayer mentions is that of Rhetoric (ages 14-16). During this period the child moves from merely grasping the logical sequence of arguments to learning how to present them in an persuasive, aesthetically pleasing form. If you would like more information on the use of the Trivium in a classical curriculum, I would invite

you   to   peruse   my   Web   page-
http://members.aol.com/Fritztutor

The second part is the Quadrivium, which is to find

one's own meaning through books, most likely ancient

writings or a vast library of literature.

CLASSICAL COURSES
Classical Languages
Greek
Latin

Art Subject
Drawing
Architecture
Design
Paint
Sculpture

Vocational Education
Animation
Office work
Paralegal
Dental Hygienist
Trades

Drama
Film
TV
Theatre
Music
Physical Education
Soccer
Archery
Gym
Aerobics
T-ball
Volleyball
Swimming
Badminton
Tennis
Fencing
Chess
Lacrosse
Golf
Basketball
Football
Volleyball

Piano
Orchestra
Choir

General Science

Zoology
Earth science
Physical science
Astronomy

Biology
Chemistry
Geology
Physics
Botany
Meteorology

Chapter 3
School description

Fig 3. *school design*

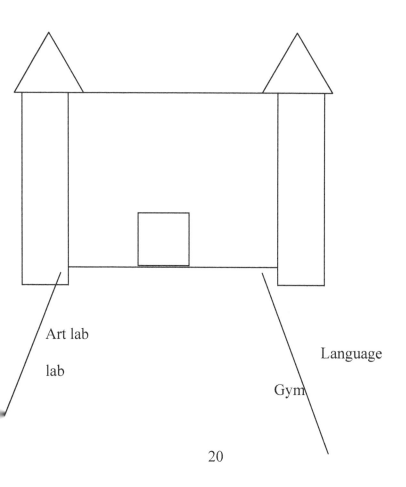

Art lab

lab

Language

Gym

School Description

Sociology classes are taught in a homeroom beginning at 8:00 am. Then students disburse to specialized labs where languages, Art, PE, Math, and Science are taught.

These labs consist of a whole wing of the school.

Figure 4. Basic School Design

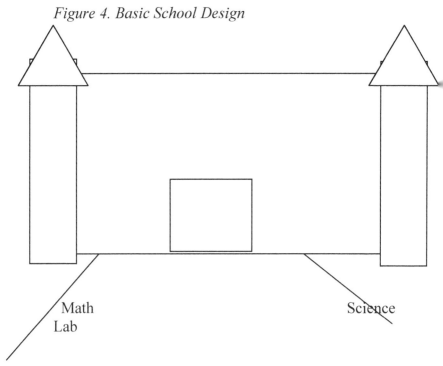

School Description

Part 1

The model campus includes the following: A recreational building including, game room, and a multi purpose room open from 6:00 am to 10:00 pm. An elementary complex includes social learning rooms for 3-year-old children and cafeterias, which can house 200 to 500 people eating at on time.

Math, Science, Art and language have wings that are auditorium sized.

For this discussion, we shall focus on the language laboratory. The projected number of patrons is 60 to 100 people daily. The laboratory will house a library full of audiovisual materials in at least four languages. The language laboratory also accommodates the language instructors and their offices. The language laboratory will be beige in

22

color to facilitate cognitive activities. Ceiling light will be 70 per cent, and wall lighting will be 40 percent. Desktop lighting will be 35 percent, and floor lighting will be no more than 30 per cent so brightness of work is no more than 10 percent. Classrooms and all outer rooms will have widows. The library won't have windows to reduce student distraction. Tables will be adjustable and light in color. Key boards, wrist support, feet rest, computer hoods, and color monitors will be used for learner comfort. Furniture will be institution quality. There will be disability ramps and front doors, including parking. All software will be checked out of the library.

Laboratory Proposal

Philosophy

The laboratories are as follows: Language, Science, and Math. The following is an example of language laboratory is an example of this area. Laboratories will be auditorium-sized halls with different spaces for hands on activities. A subject area expert will appear in person or as a cyber teacher for instruction. These auditoriums will hold as many as 60 students at a time. There will be one subject area expert per subject per time zone.

In theory one teach could teach large amounts of children around the world at one time. If a dollar amount per child is attached to each child for cost of education. The subject matter expert could make as much money as he or she wishes. Then the subject matter expert gives the children a task to perform or

24

complex problem to solve in groups. For example, the instructor could assign a robot or word problem to finish in the math lab. Of course assistants will be on hand to help the children in person observing groups or one on one.

Children need the mastery of language of any language they choose to explore. Often we need the competency of English and another language. This model introduces or revives the classics for children and produces precision in fluency. The use of technology provides children with an edge in today's industry. For example, if these children can't use a basic Windows 98 program, they may not be the one to get the job. The purpose is to prepare students for the work place.

The Sociology Instructional Design Model

Goal

The goal of this model is to provide opportunities to children from diverse and economically deprived backgrounds to learn, and to adequately train pupils for the world with technology.

Language Laboratory Objectives

1. To provide each student access to the latest resources available

2. To provide each teacher access to the latest resources available

3. To provide books that are educational

4. To provide audio visual materials

5. To provide reference books

6. To provide fiction and non- fiction books

7. To provide students a place to study quietly

8. To be a vehicle for information

9. To provide help to those in search of information

CYBER SCHOOL

In the case of overcrowding, cyber school can be used. A greater number of students from 30-50 per class can be taught with the sociology model using a cyber teacher. The cyber teacher can be utilized as a subject matter expert. He will teach the children one subject from a location on the Internet using video camera. She will dismiss the students to labs. He will have the opportunity to teach more than one class as at time from her location.

She will be paid based on vouchers totaling an estimated 3-10,000 dollars per child. This formula will also enable her to earn as much money as she wants.

Students will explore the learning labs with their teacher's assistants and return to the sociology classrooms when they are finished.

Floor Plans

Office Design *fig. 5*

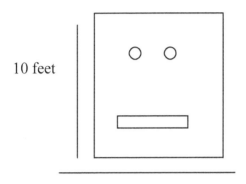

10 feet

20 feet

Audio Visual Room *fig 6*

5 feet

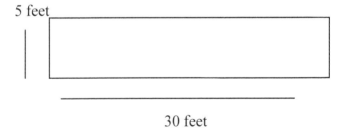

30 feet

The Sociology Instructional Design Model

Classroom *fig 7*

10 feet

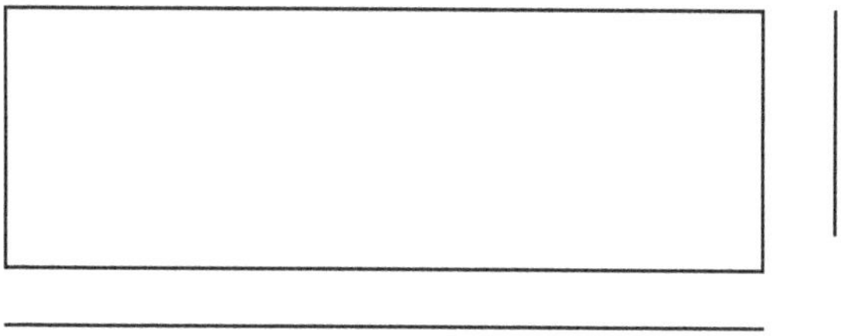

30feet

Resources Storage *fig 8*

10

feet

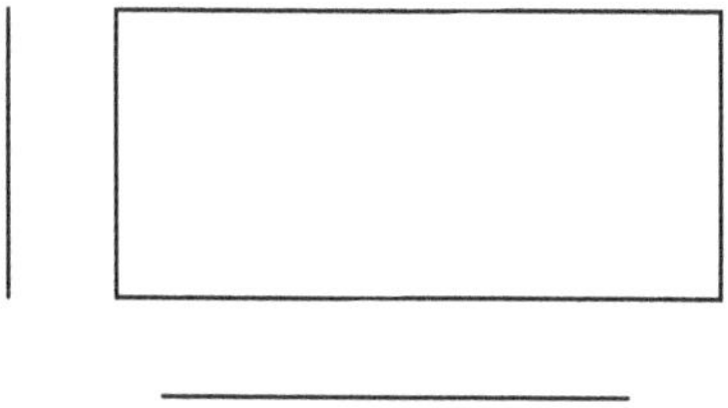

20 feet

Circular wing floor plan *fig 9.*

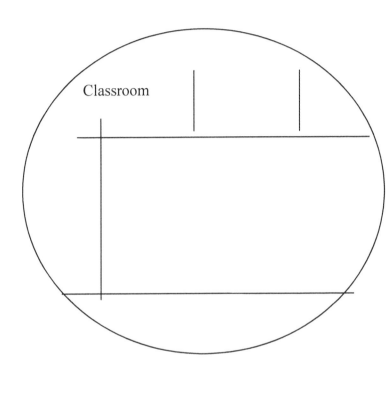

70 feet

Math Laboratory

Beginning in the 6th grade the student may pick his own courses. The college diploma consists of Algebra through Calculus. Logic and Statistics must be attempted, but only a grade of C is required in these courses. The regular diploma consists of general math through business then using the vocational education track to 12th grade.

Figure 10. Math Wing

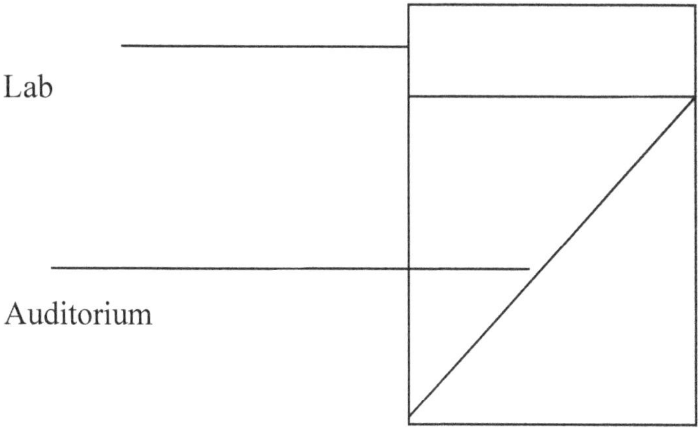

Lab

Auditorium

Math Lab Curriculum

3 years the concept of number-A survey course of introduction to numerals and integers (Webster 1991).

4 years the concept of number- A survey course of introduction to numerals and integers (Webster 1991).

Kindergarten-General Math-A course that teaches multiplication, addition, subtraction, and division (Webster 1991).

Grade 1 -General Math- A course that teaches multiplication, addition, subtraction, and division (Webster 1991).

Grade2 -General Math- A course that teaches multiplication, addition, subtraction, and division (Webster 1991).

Grade 3 -General Math- A course that teaches multiplication, addition, subtraction, and division (Webster 1991).

Grade 4 -Business Math-A course that teaches mathematics in business (Webster 1991).

Grade 5 -Problem Solving-A course that teaches students to use numbers to solve word problems (Webster 1991).

Grade 6 -Algebra-A course that teaches student to solve for x to solve problems (Webster 1991).

Grade 7 Geometry-A course that explores the branch of mathematics that deals with points, lines, angles, surfaces and solids (Webster 1991).

Grade 8 Algebra 2-The student learns a form of algebra that deals with complex equations (Webster 1991).

Grade 9 Trigonometry-This course explores a branch of mathematics that deals with the relationships between the sides and the angles of triangles, and calculations based on trigonometric functions (Webster 1991).

Grade 10 Calculus- A system of mathematics that deals with the analysis and calculation using symbolic notation (Webster 1991).

Grade 11 Statistics-Interpretation of numerical data (Webster 1991).

Grade 12 Logic-The study of reasoning (Webster 1991).

Science Laboratory

Biology, Chemistry, Physics are required for the college diploma, Biology, physical science are required for the regular diploma. The learner may choose classes beginning at grade 6.

Fig. 11 Science Wing

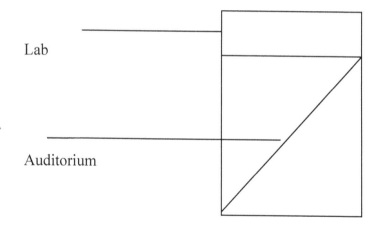

Lab

Auditorium

Science Lab Curriculum

Preschool (Seasons)-Students are introduced to seasons through play, song, and the arts.

Pre Kindergarten (animals)-In this class, students learn about various types of animals (Webster 1991).

Kindergarten-General Science- A course that explores environmental education, agriculture, Botany, and Ontology (Webster 1991).

Grade 1-General Science- A course that explores environmental education, agriculture, Botany, and Ontology (Webster 1991).

Grade 2-General Science- A course that explores environmental education, agriculture, Botany, and Ontology (Webster 1991).

Grade 3-General Science- A course that explores environmental education, agriculture, Botany, and Ontology (Webster 1991).

The Sociology Instructional Design Model

Grade 4-General Science-Process skills- This course teaches the procedures to science if discovery and method.

Grade 5-Astronomy-The study of the solar systems (Webster).

Grade 6 -Computer Science-This course is a survey, of keyboarding, software, hardware, and networking (Webster). (Webster 1991).

Grade 7 -Earth Science- A course that explores the study of our planet earth and the surface of the world (Webster 1991).

Grade 8 –Engineering-This course is a survey of basic engineering. (Webster 1991).

Grade 9 Genetics-This course surveys the human cell, and DNA (Webster 1991).

Grade 10 Biology-This course explores living things (Webster 1991).

Grade 11 Chemistry-This course introduces the learner to the composition and reactions of matter (Webster 1991).

Grade 12 Physics-This course explores the science of matter and energy and the relations between them (Webster 1991).

Physical Education Laboratory

Running, walking, swimming, health and nutrition are required for graduation in any diploma.

Recreation

Beginning with grades 1-12 the learner may pick what he or she wants to study. For example, weight training, tennis; volleyball may be taken at any time.

Figure 12. Physical Education Court

For outside games

interior

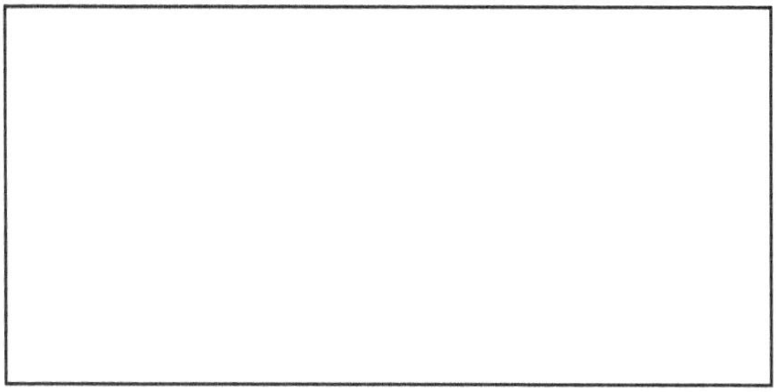

The Sociology Instructional Design Model

Recreation

3 years free play-1 organized game per week

3 years free play 2 organized games per week

5 years swimming, organized games

Grade 1 -organized games

Grade 2- organized games

Grade 3 -organized games

Grade 4 -organized games

Grade 5 -organized games

Grade 6 -organized games

Grade 7 -organized games

Grade 8- relays

Grade 9 -health and nutrition

Grade 10-weight lifting aerobics, football, and soccer

Grade 11- tennis, volley bally, and basketball

Grade 12- walking/ running

Art Laboratory

The arts are incorporated into before, after school, and camps. However the music laboratory is three stories, complete with a cathedral style concert hall on the list floor for events. The upper levels are for classrooms and instrument storage.

Figure 13. Art Wing

Art Studio Upstairs

hands

on

Laboratory

or

Instrument

room

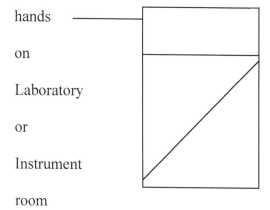

Chorus

Or

Orchestra

Auditorium

Music

Dance

Drama

Chorus

Piano

Choir

Violin

Cello

Saxophone

Bassoon

French horn

Trumpet

Trombone

Clarinet

Dance Topics

Creative Movement

Modern

Tap

Jazz

Ballet

Art Topics

Sculpting

The Sociology Instructional Design Model

Chapter 4

Staff

Social Awareness Teacher

Your child will spend most of her day with the social awareness teacher. The social awareness teacher is your contact for all purposes. As the child grows older they will depend on this teacher less and less. There are two social awareness teachers in each room. Each teacher has equal status; the class is divided up so each teacher responsible for five or six students. However, both teachers are responsible for the whole class curriculum. The social awareness teachers prepare students for the outside world. The social awareness teaches guides class changing to other classes.

The Sociology Instructional Design Model

Each teacher must teach one class per week in social studies starting in kindergarten. In preschool and Prekindergarten there is not a specific class taught, but the teacher provides an atmosphere in the classroom where students learn, season, manners, social interaction, getting along with others, and cultural aspects.

Qualifications-One teacher must be certified in special education. The other teacher may have a degree in any of the social sciences, such as psychology, sociology etc. An AA degree is required for teaching preschool, nursery, and PreK.

The Sociology Instructional Design Model

SCHEDULE

Kindergarten 10:00am-10: 30am daily

Prek 8:00am-8: 30am library

Preschool 8:30am-9:00am library

Grade 1 -11:00am

Grade 2 -11:00am

Grade3 -12:00pm

Grade 4 -12:00pm

Grade 5 -1:00pm

Grade 6 -1:00pm

Grade 7 -2:00pm

Grade 8 -2:00pm

Grade 9-12 will not have a particular library time. They will have English, one language of choice, and study hall.

The students will participate in classes from 3:00pm-6:00pm.

The Sociology Instructional Design Model

Children from grades 1-12 will participate in gym time in the morning until 10:00 am

Lunch at 11:00 am.

Children from grades 1-12 have classes from 12:00pm until 6:00pm.

One teacher will teach from 8:00am-3:00pm, 12:00pm-6:00pm, 10:00am –4:00pm

An assistant will work in the classroom from 12:00pm-6:00pm.

When the teachers are not teaching they will be taking care of administrative duties in the language laboratory.

Only one language in a specialized area will be used.

Whole School Schedule

7:00am –8:00am Fine Arts

8:00am-9:00am   Sociology (home room)

9:00am-10: 30am Math

10:30am-12:00pm Science

12:00pm-1:00pm Recess and lunch

1:00pm-2: 30pm   Language Arts

3:00pm-5:00pm   Sports

Organizational Line and Staff Chart

Fig 14.

Organizational Chart

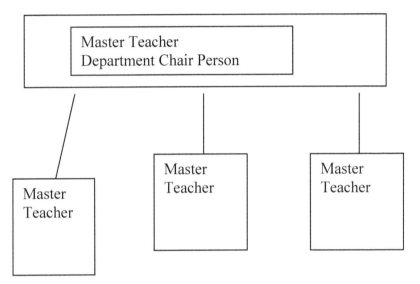

The Sociology Instructional Design Model

Personnel Job Description

Position title: Master Teacher

Department-Language Lab

Reports to: Principal or Assistant Principal

Personal Mission or Responsibilities: The master teacher is responsible for teaching classes in German for preschool through twelfth grade. The applicant must posses the ability to teach, reading, reading readiness, and pre writing skills in these areas. He or She will be responsible for cataloging, checking out books, and inventory or library materials.

Personal Skills and characteristics:

Organizer, Ability to supervise teaching assistants

Team player

Qualifications: The position requires a Bachelor of Arts degree in German. One year experience at least.

This is a salaried position with 20 hours or classroom time, and 15 hours of office duties. One hour paid break and half hour paid break in classroom hours totaling 40 hours per week.

Personnel Job Description

Position title: Master Teacher

Department-Language Lab

Reports to: Principal or Assistant Principal

Personal Mission or Responsibilities: The master teacher is responsible for teaching classes in Romance Languages for preschool through twelfth grade. The applicant must posses the ability to teach, reading, reading readiness, and pre writing skills in these areas.

He or She will be responsible for cataloging, checking out books, and inventory or library materials.

Personal Skills and characteristics:

Organizer, Ability to supervise teaching assistants

Team player

Qualifications: The position requires a Bachelor of Arts degree in Romance Languages. One year experience at least. This is a salaried position with 20 hours or classroom time, and 15 hours of office duties. One hour paid break and half hour paid break in classroom hours totaling 40 hours per week.

Personnel Job Description

Position title: Master Teacher

Department-Language Lab

The Sociology Instructional Design Model

Reports to: Principal or Assistant Principal

Personal Mission or Responsibilities: The master teacher is responsible for teaching classes in language arts and or sign language for preschool through twelfth grade. The applicant must posses the ability to teach, reading, reading readiness, and pre writing skills in these areas. He or She will be responsible for cataloging, checking out books, and inventory or library materials.

Personal Skills and characteristics:

Organizer, Ability to supervise teaching assistants

Team player

Qualifications: The position requires a Bachelor of Arts degree in Language Arts. One year experience at least. This is a salaried position with 20 hours or classroom time, and 15 hours of office duties. One hour paid break and half hour paid break in classroom hours totaling 40 hours per week.

Personnel Job Description

Position title: Teaching Assistant

Department-Language Lab

Reports to: Principal or Assistant Principal

Personal Mission or Responsibilities: The teaching assistant is responsible for helping the master teacher with their classes. He or She will be responsible for cataloging, checking out books, and inventory or library materials.

Personal Skills and characteristics:

Organizer, Ability to supervise teaching assistants

Team player

The Sociology Instructional Design Model

Qualifications: The position requires an Associates Degree. One year experience at least. This is a salaried position with 20 hours or classroom time, and 15 hours of office duties. One hour paid break and half hour paid break in classroom hours totaling 40 hours per week.

Chapter 5
SOCIOLOGY TRAINING

Sociology Training Model *fig 15.*

Anthropology
Archaeology
Civics
Psychology
Geography

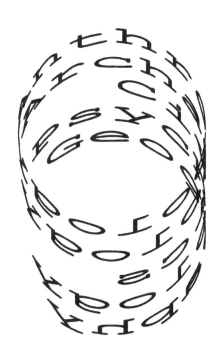

Fig. 16

**Nursery School Model
0-3 Years**

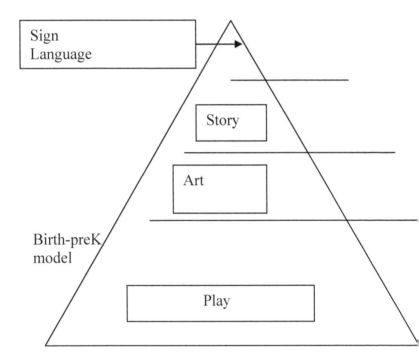

Typical Schedule

PRE   K Schedule

7:00-9:00 SQ
9:00-9:15 Circle
9:15-9:30 Break
9:30-11:30 Centers – Math, Language, technology, and Science in laboratories
12:00 Lunch
12:30-2:00 Nap
2:00-2:30-Break
2:45-3:00 Go home or after school Classical Training time.

Kindergarten Schedule

7:00-9:00 SQ
9:00-9:15 Circle
9:15-9:30 Break
9:30-11:30 Centers – Math, Language, technology, and Science in laboratories
12:00 Lunch
12:30-2:00 Nap
2:00-2:30-Break
2:45-3:00 Go home or after school Classical Training time.

SOCIAL SCIENCE CURRICULUM BY GRADE

The environments for each grade will be based on a social environment that is age appropriate for the age group present. For example, in preschool the sociology curriculum will come out of the concept of *my home* which includes comfortable spaces for the children, art on the wall, couches and lockers as a home a way from home for this homeroom.

Preschool-Sociology (My Home)

Pre Kindergarten-Sociology (The World Around US)- A survey course of human societies. (Webster 1991).

Kindergarten-Egology –This course will explore the study of one's self (Webster 1991).

Grade 1-Ettiquette (Webster 1991).

Grade 2-Anthropology-This course covers the origin and culture development of the human race (Webster 1991).

The Sociology Instructional Design Model

Grade 3-Acrheaology-The recovery and study of material evidence of human life and cultures including past ages (Webster 1991).

Grade 4-Geography- (Maps, roads etc) A survey course of the earth with an emphasis on countries (Webster 1991).

Grade 5-Sociology-Diversity-A course, which focuses on the diversity portion of sociology (Webster 1991).

Grade 6-Geography (Countries)-A survey course of the earth with an emphasis on countries (Webster 1991).

Grade 7-Civics-States- The study of duties associated with the states in the USA (Webster 1991).

Grade 8 –Civics-State History- A survey of history of the states, past civics, and citizenship (Webster 1991).

The Sociology Instructional Design Model

Grade 9-Human Behavior- How to conduct one self and function as a productive part of society (Webster 1991).

Grade 10-Civics-World History-The study of history of the whole world including past civics and citizenship of different races of past and present (Webster 1991).

Grade 11-Civics (US Histories)-The survey of history of the whole US including past civics citizenship or different races past and present (Webster 1991).

Grade 12 Psychology- This course includes the study of individuals or groups (Webster 1991).

Languages

Nursery (0-3)- Story time and Sign Language

Preschool (3 years) – Introduction to letter through art, story time, and sign language

Prekindergarten (4 years)-Introduction to letter-phonics

Kindergarten-Reading

Grade 1 -Grammar and journal

Grade 2 -Grammar and journals

Grade 3 -Grammar, journals, dictionary, and antonyms

Grade4 -Grammar (writing) poetry

Grade 5 -Stories and short stories

Grade 7 -Novels

Grade 8 -Short lessons in English

Grade 9 English 1-Introduction to writing

Grade 10 English 2-Analysisin World Literature

Grade 11 English-3-Analysis in British Literature

The Sociology Instructional Design Model

Grade 12 English 4- Analysis in United States Literature

Fluency in one other language besides English is required of two other languages.

English 4 is required for graduation.

Languages are offered in grades 3-12.

Children and their parents can pick other languages during camps.

Course Break Down:

Word tests and quizzes

Book reports

Essays

Journals

Oral speeches and presentations

References

Gagne, R.M., &Briggs, L.J. (1979) Principles of instructional design. New York: Holt, Rinehart, & Winston, 236-238.

Gardner, Howard. (1983). *Frames of Mind: The Theory of Multiple Intelligences*, NY: Basic Books

Goleman, Daniel. (1985). Emotional Intelligence, NY: Bantam Books

Hinrichs, Fritz (2006) Introduction to classical education. Resourced on July 15, 2006 http://www.gbt.org/text/intro.html

IQ (2006) Encyclopedia Britannica, Inc. Retrieved on July 15, 2006 http://www.britannica.com/eb/article-9042732

Plutarch (1871) "On Banishment," *Plutarch's Morals,* rev. William W. Goodwin, vol. 3, p. 19 (1871).

Solovey, Peter and Mayer, John D. (1990). "Emotional Intelligence," *Imagination, Cognition, and Personality* *9,* pp. 185-211

Webster-Merriam. (1991). Webster's II New Riverside Notebook Dictionary, Revised Ed.MA: Houghton Mifflin Company.